Boise State University Western Writers Series   Number 94

Charles Erskine Scott Wood

By Edwin R. Bingham

University of Oregon

Editors: Wayne Chatterton
James H. Maguire

Business Manager:
James Hadden

Cover Design and Illustration
by Arny Skov, Copyright 1990

Boise State University, Boise, Idaho

Copyright 1990
by the
Boise State University Western Writers Series

ALL RIGHTS RESERVED

Library of Congress Card No. 90-80259

International Standard Book No. 0-88430-093-5

Printed in the United States of America by
Boise State University Printing and Graphics Services
Boise, Idaho

Charles Erskine Scott Wood

Charles Erskine Scott Wood

Like a number of Western writers—Bret Harte, Mary Austin, Joaquin Miller, and Mary Hallock Foote, to name four—Charles Erskine Scott Wood came to the American West in his youth. He spent the rest of his life on the Pacific Slope—in Oregon, for more than thirty years, and then in California, where he died at Los Gatos, a month short of his ninety-second birthday. That long career has nearly as many facets as a fly's eye. West Pointer, Indian fighter, attorney, poet, artist, anarchist, satirist, land agent, lecturer, columnist, reformer, Wood was all of these and more. Indeed, he spread diverse talents and remarkable energy in such a sweeping arc that he resembles a renaissance figure out of place and out of time.

According to his good friend William Rose Benét: "Something of the largeness of the early West was in Erskine Scott Wood." True enough, but the rugged, informal, Western dimension in him was tempered by the influence of his youthful reading in classical literature that imparts an urbane and Old World flavor even to his Western verse. Moreover, his most widely read book, *Heavenly Discourse* (1927), a collection of satiric dialogues, treats *national* issues such as militarism, birth control, censorship, and fundamentalism. Wood, then, was both a Western writer and a writer in the West. However, he thought of himself first and foremost as a poet; and his major work, *The Poet in the Desert* (1913), is redolent of the southeastern Oregon landscape.

Charles Erskine Scott Wood was born on 20 February 1852 in Erie, Pennsylvania, the second son of Rosemary Carson and William Maxwell Wood, a Navy surgeon. Wood had five brothers and one sister, the youngest of the family. Wood's father was of English descent and a native of Baltimore. His mother was a Scot from Mercersburg, Pennsylvania. After the Civil War the family moved to a farm in the gently rolling hill country on the outskirts of Baltimore where, despite the taut household maintained by the senior Wood, Erskine and his brothers lived the graceful lives of a country gentleman's sons.

Wood's father used his influence to secure his second son Erskine an appointment-at-large to the United States Military Academy from President U. S. Grant. C.E. Scott Wood, as he was invariably listed on Army rolls, was an uneager cadet. He did not relish the West Point system with its unrelenting discipline and a curriculum heavily weighted on the side of mathematics and the physical sciences. In his own words, it was "work, work, work, from reveille to taps. Sunday had a brief relaxation period but it was really a study day. Saturday afternoon was a holiday for the orderly and well-behaved but I walked about every Saturday afternoon with a rifle on my shoulder for punishment." More than once C.E. Scott Wood accumulated demerits just short of the number that would bring dismissal. His academic performance, except in drawing, where he excelled, was mediocre; his military record bordered on disgrace. He never held a cadet rank. All in all, his cadet years were unnaturally formal, gallingly restrictive, and depressingly drab—a time to be resented and endured, and little more.

Upon graduation in 1874, the newly minted second lieutenant was assigned to frontier duty at Fort Bidwell in northeastern California. After some months his company was ordered to Vancouver Barracks in Washington Territory. On the long march between posts

Lieutenant Wood was fascinated by the Oregon high desert, a fascination that lasted most of his life. From Vancouver, Wood led a small exploratory probe of Alaska from which he was called back to his post in the spring of 1877 to serve as aide to General Oliver O. Howard in the campaign to force the Nez Perce Indians on to a reservation at Lapwai, Idaho Territory. Lt. Wood's moving summary of Chief Joseph's sentiments when he surrendered at Bear Paw Mountain, Montana Territory, in the fall of 1877, is quoted in whole or in part in many textbooks of United States history. The next year, Wood took part in putting down an outbreak of the Paiutes and Bannocks, and then was sent to Washington, D.C., with special dispatches. While there he married Nannie Moale Smith, his sweetheart of cadet days, on 26 November 1878. He brought his bride to Vancouver Barracks where their son Erskine was born a year later.

When General Howard was appointed superintendent of West Point in 1880, C.E. Scott Wood went with him as adjutant. On one of Mark Twain's periodic visits to the Academy, Wood extended him the hospitality of the school and agreed to publish secretly on the academy press the humorist's infamous, unsigned *1601, Conversation as it was by the Social Fireside in the Time of the Tudors*, an exercise in scatology. A second child, Nan, was born at West Point in 1882.

By this time, C.E. Scott Wood had had enough of a career not of his choosing and he was eying the law as a means of escape from the Army. He wangled a leave of absence that permitted him to take degrees in law and political science from Columbia University. While in New York, Erskine joined a circle of artists including J. Alden Weir, son of his drawing instructor at West Point; Olin Warner, sculptor of the doors of the Library of Congress; A.W. Drake, art editor of *Century*; Childe Hassam; and occasionally, Albert Pinkham Ryder. The group often met at a little French restaurant on the south side of Washington Square or at a saloon, on the corner of Fourth and Fourteenth, that served imported German beer and fine swiss cheese and rye. The talk was usually of art and the rebellion against the Hudson River school of painting. Wood was at home among those rebels who enjoyed good food and drink and heady conversation.

In 1884, First Lieutenant C.E. Scott Wood resigned his commission and entered the practice of law in Portland. There three more children were born: Maxwell, Berwick, and Lisa. Portland was Wood's home for thirty-four years. He specialized in maritime and corporation law; he also served as land agent for Lazard Freres, a New York banking and investment firm, overseeing the Willamette Valley and Cascade Mountain wagon road grant that stretched from Albany, Oregon, to the Idaho border. At the same time he served propertied clients, Erskine worked the other side of the tracks, defending radicals and feminists like Emma Goldman, Margaret Sanger, and the "Wobblies." Erskine's avocations were writing and painting. To facilitate this creative work he maintained a secret office in the Chamber of Commerce building removed from his law office. He wrote essays and short stories on radical themes for Louis Post's *Public* (Chicago) and Benjamin Tucker's *Liberty* (New York). He was also a major contributor for more than a decade to *Pacific Monthly*, a literary and promotional magazine out of Portland. C.E.S. Wood became a kind of unofficial arbiter of taste and culture. He encouraged wealthy Oregonians to buy the work of American painters like Ryder and Hassam. He himself painted in oil and paste.

In 1901 *A Book of Tales* was printed privately in Portland on a small hand press. These are Indian legends that Erskine gathered during his frontier experiences, with a concluding myth of his own devising.

In 1910, Erskine met a young poet, Sara Bard Field Ehrgott, who saw great promise in his collection of poetic stanzas descriptive of the Oregon high desert, a collection which he had given the uninspired title "Civilization." Together they worked to shape the pieces into *Poet in the Desert*, first published in Portland in 1915. The two poets became lovers as well as collaborators.

About the same time, Colonel Wood (the rank was a militia title conferred by an Oregon governor) wrote a brief, satiric dialogue poking fun at Anthony Comstock, that roundsman of the Lord, and his efforts to suppress Margaret Sanger's birth control movement. Erskine sent the dialogue to *The Masses*, a New York monthly of radical writing. Editors Max Eastman and Floyd Dell took it and asked for more. Wood obliged. *The Masses* carried a number of the dialogues but when, in late 1917, the magazine was suppressed by the government for alleged interference with the war effort, the editors returned to Erskine the dialogues they had not yet published.

In 1918, Colonel Wood concluded long-term negotiations for the sale of the sprawling wagon road grant to Louis Hill, son of James J. Hill, for which he received a million-dollar commission. This sale enabled Wood to retire from law practice at age sixty-six, to break with his family after setting up trust funds for their financial support, and to relocate in northern California with Sara Bard Field, who had divorced her husband.

The two poets lived in San Francisco for a time and then, in 1924, fleeing fog and people, they built a house on a hill in Los Gatos. There they established a kind of pastoral salon where they entertained guests and staged celebrations of weddings and birthdays and other milestones. More or less frequent visitors to "The Cats," as they called their hillside retreat, included Robin and Una Jeffers, Mark Van Doren, Lincoln and "Peter" (Steffens's pet name for his wife, Ella Winter) Steffens, Yehudi Menuhin, Ansel Adams, John Steinbeck, and William Rose Benét.

Erskine gathered the handful of dialogues *The Masses* editors had returned to him, added to them, and Vanguard Press published the lot in 1927 as *Heavenly Discourse*. The satiric dialogues went through some forty printings and there was a Penguin paperback edition in 1946.

In 1931, Wood published *Too Much Government*, social and political comment with a libertarian theme; in 1937 *Earthly Discourse*, much less effective than its celestial predecessor. In 1938, after his first wife's death, Erskine and Sara were married.

Charles Erskine Scott Wood died in January 1944. His ashes were sown through the live oak grove at "The Cats" as he had wished.

C.E.S. Wood followed a long trail on his way to becoming a writer. Ironically, the father who assumed he had launched his second son safely on an army career through the appointment to the United States Military Academy, provided a model for Erskine, whose literary aspirations ran contrary to a military career. Surgeon Wood had published graceful accounts of his duty with the Asiatic squadron in Siam and China and with the Pacific fleet off Mexico. Moreover, the son read avidly in the father's library of English, French, and Spanish classics. Even at West Point, Cadet Wood (despite the rigor of the regimen) had found time to read the novels of William Gilmore Simms, Bulwer Lytton, and Sir Walter Scott as well as parts of Spenser, Chaucer, and Shakespeare. Thus he drew upon his small reservoir of private time to redress the lack of literary and humanistic emphasis in the West Point course of study and in the process he gratified the normal urge of an aspiring writer to read the works of successful authors. Off and on the young cadet also kept a journal in which, among other things, he recorded his progress in courting Nannie Moale Smith.

The first hard evidence that C.E. Scott Wood harbored literary ambitions came in a series of stern, measured reprimands from Dr. Wood in response to the young cadet's repeated expressions of a restless desire to escape the West Point system. At one time cadet Wood threatened to resign and offer his services to the Mexican army; at another he contemplated escaping to Florida to grow oranges. Most persistently, however, the unhappy cadet expressed a longing to embark on a literary career as a means of avoiding a life in the Army with its low pay and slow advancement. Dr. Wood's response was calm but caustic. He reminded his son of the honor and security that went with the soldier's profession and chided him for considering making literature a trade. "If one has the abilities for literary production," he wrote, "he owes the use of them to the world, and these rewards come, as should all honors, unsought." The elder Wood painted a grim picture of the grinding life of a literary hack, concluding on what for him was a light note: "I think if you reflect upon this letter, you will be amused by your crazy notion that to be a literary man you must change a profession, or rather that your genius will be more fertile when you do not know where to get your breakfast . . . . If this letter had been written as an essay for a magazine I could get five dollars a magazine page for it and maybe you may lay it in store as the basis of your future experience in literary labor."

In the final letter he wrote to his son at West Point Dr. Wood advised the cadet ". . . to abandon all feverish and restless desire after change and address yourself with honest and unceasing vigilance to the labor, the claims and obligations of the present around you—and of the place and position to which you are called." Evidently Dr. Wood's continuous counsel prevailed for when the West Point class of 1874 was graduated, reduced from an entering strength of sixty-seven to forty-four, the rebellious Wood stood academically squarely in the middle. However, Erskine's literary impulse smouldered rather than died.

Service on the Far Western frontier, beginning at Fort Bidwell in 1875, rekindled the young lieutenant's interest in writing. He sent a manuscript to his brother Maxwell at the Navy department in Washington, D.C., requesting that Max try to place it with *Harper's* or *Scribner's*. Max wrote Erskine at Bidwell with the bad news that neither editor was interested. The letter is tantalizing in that Max describes the manuscript only as being "too deep for the reading public." He goes on to encourage his younger brother to turn to lighter, more attractive subjects growing out of experiences and materials close at hand: "There are two officers here now who are writing little sketches in which they lay the scenes among some of the *funnier ports* they have visited. They bring in a little mirth, a little love, etc. and a good deal of fiction and get $10.00 a page from the magazine publishers. One of them illustrates his story. Do this. Don't write trash . . . . Cultivate a style of your own—concise free and simple and after you have made a little money and reputation and gained a little more experience and a few more years you can branch out into deeper subjects."

It was sound advice and Erskine resumed the journal he had kept at West Point. Still, Bidwell was scarcely the kind of station that invited literary exploitation. True, as recently as 1873, troops from the post had participated in the Modoc War, but by the time Lt. Wood reached the fort all was tranquil on the Far Western frontier and remained so during his brief stay.

Action of a sort came when Wood's Company H received orders transferring it to Fort Vancouver on the north side of the lower Columbia River in Washington Territory, headquarters for the

Department of the Pacific. Early in August 1875, the soldiers set off north and west across the lonely stretches of southeastern Oregon. In his journal Lt. Wood recorded fully the impact of that march. So much of sun, silence, and space was new to a boy from the shores of Erie and the back country of Baltimore. The world of his youth had been green and wooded, with water, either fresh or salt, ever close at hand and part of his life. His memories of fishing and exploring sorties on Presque Isle or of possum hunts in the Maryland woods recall a cozy and intimate environment where the vistas were lovely but limited; where one could enter into a comfortable collaboration with one's surroundings. Now, on the far edge of the West, Wood was learning a new conception of space and scale. Man was minuscule. In most directions, the land lay flat and monotonous all the way to the horizon. Later he called the Oregon desert a "lean and stricken land." Yet within the region there is relief from rimrock, rabbit bush, juniper, and sage. Two lakes, Malheur and Harney, separated by a narrow bar, provide a vast area of tule marsh, interconnecting waterways, and wild meadows that furnish food, nest material, and perfect cover for more than two hundred species of waterfowl and wild birds. After the troops made camp, Lieutenant Wood rambled wide-eyed through the marsh that fluttered with movement and rang with song—the sibilant notes of blackbirds like air blown through a dusty flute, the muffled pile-driver boom of the bittern, the sharp, mewing cry of curlew and gull, the plaintive, monotonous call of the killdeer, and other noises too muted or confused or unfamiliar for the young officer to sort out and identify. In a spot where the matted sedge thinned, he counted more than thirty sandhill crane feeding in the shallow water. One species of wader caught Wood's attention with its curved bill and its brilliant, gleaming upper parts of iridescent green and purple and bronze. He shot two of them, stretching the skins to dry in the sun, with the thought that he would send them to decorate the summer hats of his Baltimore sweetheart when he reached Fort Vancouver. That night Lieutenant C.E. Scott Wood lay sleepless, sensing the isolation, the solitude and hush, and above all the vastness of the landscape and the magnificent sweep of the dark dome above him with its bursts of stars. As the camp noises faded, a small owl, puffed up and mottled like a partridge, mounted a badger mound and stood solemn and still on legs toothpick thin and long enough to seem borrowed. For some time the owl stood silent and then began its song, a high, tremulous, mellow *coo-coo-hoo*, much like a dove but higher, fainter, little more than a murmur. Years later Colonel Wood recorded with sensitive precision his memory of that night on the Harney Desert and the soothing serenade of the burrowing owl. That first encounter with the Harney Desert while he was en route to Fort Vancouver, worked profoundly on Erskine's imagination and would in time inspire his finest poetry.

 C.E.S. Wood's writing first saw print in the July 1882 number of *Century Magazine* and was evidence that he had taken brother Max's advice to heart. Wood spun a tale of his adventures in Alaska in the early spring of 1875. The piece, "Among the Tlingits of Alaska," is a colorful amalgam of fact and fancy, heavily illustrated with engravings provided by the magazine's editor. Toward the end of the story, Lt. Wood renders this "Song of the Salmon Fishing" that he alleges was sung to him by a "Chilkaht" maiden:

 Why is the young man sorrowful?
 Oh why is the young man sad?
 Ah-ka. His maiden has left him.
 The long suns have come,
 The ice now is melting;
 Now comes the salmon

He leaps in the river,
In the moon's gentle twilight
He throws up a bow—
A bow of bright silver.
Lusty and strong he darts through the water,
He sports with his mate;
He springs from the water.
All the dark season
He has lain hidden.
Now he comes rushing.
And ripples the river.
Purple and gold, and red and bright silver
Shine on his sides and flash in his sporting.
How he thrashes the net!
How he wrenches the spear!
But the red of his sides
Is stained with a redder;
The maid of the young man leans o'er the salmon
White laugh her teeth,
Clear rings her laughter;
Which passes canoes all busy and happy,
Which outstrips the noise of the many mixed voices
And pierces the heart of her sorrowful lover.
She has forgot him,
She joys with another.
All for another she chases the salmon,
Ah-ka. Your sweetheart has left you.
So they do jeer him,
Ah-ka—your sweetheart is here at the fishing!
Ah-ka—how like you this gay salmon season?
"Among the Tlingits in Alaska" was the July *Century's* lead arti-

cle and is typical of the kind of writing about the American West so frequently featured in established Eastern magazines in the Gilded Age. Moreover, "Song of the Salmon Fishing" is likely the first piece of poetry Wood published.

Between May 1884 and July 1893, *Century* carried three more Far Western pieces resting on Wood's Army experiences: one deals with Chief Joseph, famous Nez Perce leader; one with an Indian horse race; and one is a collection of profiles of Indian chiefs. The first of these is particularly significant because it contains the surrender speech of Chief Joseph at Bear Paw Mountain in Montana Territory on 5 October 1877. That speech is among the most memorable statements in the history of Indian-white relations in North America. It rings true to the tradition of Native American oratory. However, the fact is, that in all likelihood Joseph uttered not a word when he handed over his rifle to Colonel Nelson Miles. It was Lt. Wood, acting as General Howard's aide-de-camp, who composed the famous speech and reported it as coming from Joseph's lips. It was not simply a matter of on-the-spot improvisation. Lt. Wood, two of General Howard's Nez Perce scouts—Old George and Captain John—and interpreter Joseph Chapman had visited the Nez Perce camp that morning, October fifth, to make preliminary arrangements for a formal surrender. At that time Chief Joseph put together his reply to the Army's insistence that he come to terms. He expressed sorrow over the loss of the chiefs, particularly his beloved brother Ollokot. He voiced concern over the fate of those of his people who already had fled. He noted the freezing cold and the lack of blankets. "I am tired; my heart is sick and sad," he said. These sentiments and comments were fragments of what a short time later Lt. Wood rendered as a compact, eloquent statement delivered in the Army's camp by a weeping Captain John to Howard and Miles and translated by interpreter Chapman. As a budding writer, the young aide might well have applied continuity and polish to Chapman's version of the message. It is clear that Joseph was not present at the time and that no such speech was delivered toward sunset when Joseph formally capitulated. Nevertheless, the speech is worth quoting in its more accurate if less dramatic context. The setting was Miles' camp at about 2:00 o'clock in the afternoon:

Tell General Howard I know his heart. What he told me before, I have it in my heart. I am tired of fighting. Our chiefs are killed. Looking Glass is dead. Toohoolhoolzote is dead. The old men are all dead. It is the young men who say, "Yes" or "No." He who led the young men [Ollokot] is dead. It is cold and we have no blankets. The little children are freezing to death. My people, some of them, have run away to the hills, and have no blankets, no food. No one knows where they are—perhaps freezing to death. I want to have time to look for my children, and see how many of them I can find. May be I shall find them among the dead. Hear me, my chiefs! I am tired. My heart is sick and sad.

From where the sun now stands I will fight no more forever.

The question remains who deserves the most credit for the moving statement? Is it Chief Joseph or Chapman or Wood himself? At this remove there can be no unequivocal answer. However, it is true that Chief Joseph and Wood became friends and remained so until Joseph died in 1904. Moreover, neither Joseph nor Chapman seems to have repudiated Wood's rendering of the famous speech. At any rate, it is clearly the most enduring bit of prose to emerge from the dramatic and tragic contest between the U.S. Army and the Nez Perce (See Haruo Aoki's 1989 essay).

After six years of Army service in the Far West, C.E. Scott Wood returned to West Point when General O.O. Howard assumed the superintendency of the Military Academy early in 1881, and Wood was shortly made adjutant.

Late in February, Mark Twain and Joe Twichell, Hartford's red-blooded Congregationalist minister, visited West Point. As adjutant and aide to the superintendent, Lieutenant Wood had a part in showing Twain and Twichell around the Academy and it is not difficult to imagine the young officer's delight in the chance for personal contact with the reknowned writer. This was the start of a relationship that, though but sparingly nourished by either personal contact or regular correspondence over the years, was more than casual and was highly prized by Wood until he died in 1944, nearly thirty-five years after the death of Mark Twain.

The two men met at very different stages in their careers. Mark Twain, in his mid-forties, was at the peak of his powers. Behind him were *Innocents Abroad, Roughing It, Tom Sawyer,* and *The Prince and the Pauper,* while *Life on the Mississippi* and *Huckleberry Finn* were in process. He was the most sought-after literary figure in the country, and the visit to West Point was an interesting but minor incident in a busy life. On the other hand, Lieutenant Wood, just turned twenty-nine, was virtually unknown, although his urge to write was strong. At any rate, Wood lost no time in improving the situation when he wrote Twain right after the latter's departure, enclosing an Academy publication that the humorist had requested and expressing the hope that when Twain came back for the graduation exercises in June, he might "see fit" to allow Mrs. Clemens to accompany him. This led to other letters and when Twain returned to West Point he was housed under Wood's roof.

The most tangible result of the Twain-Wood relationship was the sub rosa printing of *1601*, Twain's notorious fugitive piece of rough-and-tumble dialogue. Adjutant Wood did the job right, putting together a small but sumptuous edition on deckle-edged velum wet in mild coffee to suggest age and using Old English style type that lends a touch of elegance to the four-letter words. This "secret" Academy printing of *1601* circulated among the Army "brass." One copy went to John Hay and another to the Bishop of London. For a time Erskine and Twain exchanged letters and the humorist's influence can be seen in Wood's writing style, both in his published work and his correspondence.

By the turn of the century, Charles Erskine Scott Wood was well established in Portland in the practice of maritime and corporation law. At the same time, his writing career was proceeding apace and on several fronts. For a while he turned from Western topics to current affairs, imperialism in particular. He found outlets for his poetry in liberal and libertarian journals such as Louis Post's *Public* and Benjamin Tucker's *Liberty*. In conventional but stridently satirical verse, Wood decried American Manifest Destiny in the Philippines, wrote a tribute to the Boer leader De Wet, and excoriated Joseph Chamberlain, the British imperialist statesman.

Erskine gained a local vehicle for his literary talent when Portland's *Pacific Monthly* was launched in the fall of 1898. Although it never really rivaled Boston's venerable and prestigious *Atlantic*, the *Pacific Monthly* was the leading literary magazine in the Northwest for more than a decade.

Between 1904 and 1911, the years of Erskine's deepest involvement in the magazine, he appeared 136 times writing under several pen names as well as his own. Although he spilled more ink (particularly in "Impressions," his monthly column of opinion) on national and ideological topics than on regional subjects, still Oregon and the American West figured prominently in his work. In the arena of politics, national and Western issues converged. Wood was writing at the height of the Progressive movement, with its battery of political innovations such as the initiative, referendum, and recall, measures known collectively as the "Oregon System." Like his fellow Oregonian, William S. U'Ren, the leading architect of direct legislation in the Pacific Northwest, Wood was more radical than most Progressives. For example, both he and U'Ren saw the Initiative Amendment as an instrument to achieve extreme political reform such as Henry George's single tax. However, Wood pragmatically subordinated his professed philosophical anarchism to an essentially democratic faith in the right and the capacity of ordinary citizens to govern themselves. Thus he gave spirited and reiterated support to "Statement #1," U'Ren's ingenious device to gain direct election of United States senators, a plan put forward a dozen years before passage of the Seventeenth Amendment. Further, Wood worked for the rest of the Progressive agenda—the Referendum, Recall, Direct Primary, and Women's Suffrage, although he was shrewd enough to know that none of them was a panacea.

In quite a different mood, Wood wrote a paean to Oregon's weather and to the natural beauty of the Pacific Northwest. In this brief passage he sounds very much like Charles F. Lummis in Los Angeles writing at about the same time in *Out West* and celebrating the glories of southern California. Here is Wood defending his adopted region:

> I have no apologies for our rain. It is liquid silver and it silvers the whole landscape. Through it the hills fade to delicate shadows; earth and sky are one, and all of silver. Come up in the Wintertime and see us, you crepe-skinned mummies from the lower regions, and get an Oregon complexion.

In like vein Wood wrote on Portland's Festival of Roses in 1908, including in his essay a bit of the early history of the city along with his own recollections of Portland in the 1870s and '80s. A preservationist ahead of his times, Erskine went on to deplore the commercial assault on old-growth timber:

> It seems to me that this great beauty and solemnity is perhaps as valuable as the shriek and clamor of the mill. It is a pity to have all this majesty of antiquity wholly destroyed. Man cannot restore it. It cannot be built by Nature herself in less than a thousand years, nor indeed ever, for it never is renewed the same . . . . There is no spot where the primeval forest is assured from the attack of that worst of all microbes, the dollar.

The promotional piece concludes with Erskine's tribute to the great snow giants of the Cascades: "Jefferson to the south [of Portland]; Hood full in front; St. Helens, also full before us, like a pearly bubble of the world, and above the horizon the peaks of Rainier on the Sound and Adams away up in the Yakima country."

Aside from "Impressions," Erskine contributed verse and short stories to *Pacific Monthly*, many of them on Western themes. Under his own name he wrote conventional lyrics in the form of sonnets or songs. The last of ten sonnets celebrating the southeastern Oregon desert, appearing in the *Pacific Monthly* early in 1910, hints at the more impressive work to come in Wood's *The Poet in the Desert:*

Lean, barren Desert, gray as any nun,
Up-riven rocks and silver leagues of sage;
The scarred old Mother, sere in countless age,
With naked breast parched dry beneath the sun.
And so it was when Time was first begun;
No blot of Man, no change upon thy page,
No cry for pity, since God in his rage
Set Desolation's seal thy brow upon.
Brave solitude, there's Freedom in thy breath
Which kissed eternity, and sweet release
From teasing strife and heart-corroding cares,

From out thy temples, stealing unawares,
There comes unto my troubled soul a peace
Wide as thy grandeur and as deep as Death.

Between September 1908 and November 1911, Erskine published a dozen poems about the American West under the pseudonym William Maxwell. These were romantic ballads exploiting familiar themes of love, betrayal, danger, and death set in mining and cow camp. There are señoritas and troopers, a grim tale of drought, and a hopeful verse on irrigation. Southwestern desert scenes are prominent. The verse is sentimental, often melodramatic, not worth quoting.

Pacific Monthly carried fourteen of Erskine's short stories, only one of which was under Wood's own name. All but two of the remaining thirteen bore the exotic nom de plume Felix Benguiat. Only three of the fourteen were Western stories. One, signed Orrin Seaman, was a ghost story set in an Oregon timber cruiser's cabin. "The Juniper Post" by Felix Benguiat is an anti-imperialist tale with a happy ending when a ranchwoman's young son fighting in the Philippines who is reported dead by the War Department returns, very much alive, to the desert ranch and a grieving mother. The last of Wood's Westerns, "The Toast," again by Benguiat, appeared in the magazine in November of 1908. The toast is proposed at a San Francisco banquet by a beautiful young Western woman in the form of an extended story designed to discomfit a wealthy Eastern tycoon eager to persuade her to marry him and his money. Her story is about a cowboy, Curtin St. John, who rescues her from a runaway team in the Western desert. Hers is the classic depiction of a cowboy made familiar five years earlier by Owen Wister: " . . . he moved about, skillful, self-reliant and quiet. He was tall and spare . . . the hawk type, but with no cruelty in eyes or mouth . . . brave with the strong and tender with the weak; . . . honest as the mountains, or the sea, or the desert; . . . clean inside and out; fearless, truthful, brave, honest, gentle . . . . And on whatever lonely *mesa* he may happen to be tonight, here is to Curtin St. John, Gentleman."

Early in 1909, *Pacific Monthly* carried Erskine's brief but informed essay on the paintings of the Boston impressionist Childe Hassam whose work was on exhibition in the Portland Art Museum. The piece was illustrated with four of twenty-seven canvasses painted in Harney County over two months while Hassam was the guest of Wood and Bill Hanley, the leading cattleman in the region. Erskine's conviction that the Oregon high desert would provide Hassam with a landscape worthy of the painter's brush proved correct.

For more than ten years, *Pacific Monthly* provided a convenient and appropriate outlet for C.E.S. Wood's writing. With the exception of Jack London's *Martin Eden*, the magazine's greatest literary coup, Erskine's work was on a par with that of other contributors such as George Sterling, William Rose Benét, John Muir, William McLeod Raine, Mary Austin, David Starr Jordan, and Eugene Manlove Rhodes. However, Wood was more versatile and more ubiquitous than any other writer for the magazine. His editorial voice in "Impressions" was that of a Western Progressive with a decidedly radical edge. As a convert to the Pacific Northwest he wrote of Portland with the passion of a promoter. Most of his short fiction was fanciful and exotic. In his Western verse he either recited a romantic tale or portrayed natural phenomena in sonnet or song. In almost everything he wrote he implied or decried the unfairness of the prevailing economic and political system, urging the minimalization of government and the removal of inhibitions on social and individual freedoms. In short, he was much closer to Henry George or Emma Goldman than to Hiram Johnson or Teddy Roosevelt.

At about the same time Wood began his association with *Pacific Monthly*, he found an unusual way to publish a cluster of nineteen Indian legends he had collected during Army service on the frontier. Wood's second son Maxwell and Maxwell's chum Lewis A. McArthur (later to be compiler of the superlative reference work, *Oregon Geographic Names*) operated a tiny printing shop in the attic of the McArthur home where, from time to time, they published a weekly newspaper, *The Bee*. In the winter of 1897-98, Erskine suggested to the two fourteen-year-olds that they make a small book, fashioned after the style of William Morris, from the nineteen short legends plus a longer fanciful story of his own "born of the longing of the heart," to make an even twenty. The printing was completed in the summer of 1901 as *A Book of Tales* in an edition of 105.

Wood introduced each myth by describing where he heard it and identifying his informant: the Tlingit Ta-ah-nah-klekh; Debes, a Klamath; John McBean and James Reuben, Army scouts; and Sarah Winnemucca of the Paiutes. The tales, "heard in canoe, on horseback and by the camp-fire," deal with mythic Indian characters like Yehl of the Northwest coast people or the ubiquitous Coyote. They tell of how the Cayuse got fire, how the Chilkaht River came to be, how salmon came to the Klamath. Erskine retells the stories simply, much as white writers have traditionally treated native narratives, yet at times he turns a phrase peculiarly his own. There is more romance than ethnology in *A Book of Tales*, yet the settings and the use of Indian names are truly of the West. A reviewer in the *New York Times* notes that Wood sometimes gives the tales "touches of beauty that Indian originals do not always possess" (18 August 1929: 18). Today, the 1901 edition is rare and the 1929 Vanguard Press edition under the slightly revised title *A Book of Indian Tales* is no longer in print.

Three years after *A Book of Tales* C.E.S. Wood published *A Masque of Love*, a book containing three short plays, each exploring a different aspect of love. The first play is a paean to innocent, idyllic love; the second treats of profane love and involves adultery and murder; and the third celebrates a conventional conjugal relationship in a bucolic setting. The dialogue is broken from time to time by songs in the mode of Shakespearean comedy. Now and then *A Masque of Love* is Whitmanesque: "Dead! gone back unto the cool, caressing grass, the kind, slow sisterhood of weeds." But for the most part the writing is archaic, reflecting Erskine's reading in seventeenth-century English literature. As poet-critic Genevieve Taggard observes in *American Review:* "When Mr. Wood writes under the influence of the Elizabethans, however well, I feel that he is expressing his early environment, rather than himself" (July-Aug. 1925: 416). Only in his loving reflection of nature does Wood presage the imagery he later develops when he shifts his focus to the West.

In 1910, Wood met Sara, the young woman mentioned earlier, who worked an influence on his writing and who ultimately changed his life. Sara Bard Field Ehrgott, wife of a Baptist minister, had come to Portland with her husband from Cleveland, where she had played a small role in the reform administration of Mayor Tom Johnson. Earlier she had studied briefly with Thomas R. Lounsberry, Professor of Literature at Yale, and she was writing poetry. She and Erskine met at a dinner given by Clarence Darrow on one of his trips to Portland. Similar interests in social reform and poetry led to other meetings, and a friendship developed rapidly. One day Erskine asked Sara to look through his writing stored in a chest in a corner of his private office. Near the bottom she uncovered a notebook full of free verse sketches of the desert that made the search worthwhile.

From the time of his Army service on the desert's edge, Wood had returned again and again to that "lean and stricken land." For him no fragrance matched the spicy scent of sagebrush after rain. In the desert he found freedom and proportion and peace. The desert's blinding light, its rimrock ramparts, its crags and pillars of basalt or obsidian—bare monuments in a barren waste—its wide-arching skies, all were intoxicating beyond green forest or restless sea. Sara saw great promise in the notebooks' material and the two poets worked to give structure and cohesion to the passages of varying length and merit. The result was *Poet in the Desert*, published first in 1915. There were three more editions of the long poem. All versions reveal the continuous struggle within Wood between poet and propagandist. In a cheap 1918 edition the special pleading was muted at Sara's insistence and Erskine worked for smoother articulation of the poem's parts. This edition was reprinted in 1949 in Sara Bard Field's *Collected Poems of Charles Erskine Scott Wood*, and is the one relied upon in the discussion that follows.

The long poem is divided into fifty-two parts, or cantos, of varying length. Some are dialogues between the poet and an abstraction—Truth; some resemble psalms, others sermons; some describe landscape and wild life on the high desert of Harney County in southeastern Oregon. There are melodramatic vignettes of sweatshop and mine. The Poet weeps over the betrayal of young women forced to sell "the inestimable godhood of their bodies." One canto defiantly celebrates bastardy; another exposes the obscenity of war; in yet another the poet sings of longshoremen laboring at city docks and "showing brawny breasts" and "the silken play of muscles." The whole poem is instinct with the poet's delight and awe of Nature in her infinite variety.

In an extended opening passage, a kind of prologue, the Poet is alternately defiant and diffident: "I will refuse to be molded in the common mold; / To step regularly according to custom / .... I will wander imperiously, destroying the paths, / The molds, and the patterns." But, "I have come to lose myself in immensity / and to know my littleness."

Then, in some of the best writing of his career, Wood evokes his beloved desert:

Behold the signs of the Desert:
A buzzard afloat on airy seas,
Alone between two infinities,
As I am alone between two infinities;
A juniper tree on a rocky hillside,
Dark signal, calling from afar off,
That the weary may rest in shade;
A basaltic cliff, embroidered with lichens,
Illumined by the sun, orange and yellow,
The work of a great painter,
Careless in the splash of his brush.
An ocean of sagebrush which dimly breaks
Against a purple coast too far away;
White alkali flats, shimmering as
A mirage of beautiful blue lakes,
Constantly retreating.

Behold the signs of the Desert:
The stagnant water-hole, trampled with hoofs;
About it shine the white bones of those
Who came too late.
A whirling dust-pillar, waltz of Wind and Earth;
Glistening black walls of obsidian
Where the wild tribes fashioned their arrowheads.

27

The ground with fragments is strewn,
Just as they dropped them,
The strokes of the makers undimmed
Through the dumb and desperate years;
But the hunters have gone forever.

Silence invincible; impregnable;
Compelling the soul to stand forth
And be questioned.
Night overwhelms me.
I look up to the stars,
Knowing to them my life is not
More valuable than that of the flowers;
The little, delicate flowers of the Desert,
Which, like a breath, catch at the hem of Spring
And are gone.

In another mood, the Poet traces the coming of Dawn the "life renewer, bringer of new hope" on the desert:

The prowler of the night,
The lean coyote,
Slips to his rocky fastnesses,
And noiselessly, through the gray sage,
Jack-rabbits shuttle.
Now, from the castellated cliffs,
Rock-ravens launch their proud black sails.
Wild horses neigh and toss their manes,
Trooping back to pasture;
Orioles begin to twitter.
All shy things, breathless, watch
The thin, white skirts of Dawn,
The dancer of the sky,

Tripping daintily down the roseate mountain,
Emptying a golden basin.
A red-bird, dipped in sunrise,
Cracks from a poplar top
His exultant whip above a silver world.

The Poet sees the desert as a lovely and imperious woman, of various moods and guises—princess, queen, courtesan, nun—constant only in her demand for freedom. Toward the close of the prologue the Poet calls forth the image of Truth and, through the long series of poetic passages that follow, the Poet seeks to weigh the life man has made in bondage against the life Nature makes in freedom.

Well into the poem Wood succinctly advances his anarchistic credo: "This is the pedigree of Degradation: / Authority, father of Laws; / Laws, father of Privilege; / Privilege, father of Poverty; / Poverty, father of Degradation."

In a gentle hymn to Nature, rich in imagery and restrained in statement, Wood likens rain to "the very wine of days" and concludes:

Nature has laid her finger on her lips.
Night and day she teaches that Beauty is her state,
Silence her delight
And Freedom her condition.
After Man has shouted his cries
And fretted the air with his clamor,
Lo, he lies down, also, to the great Silence,
And is gathered up again by the patient roots
Into larger beauty.

Toward the close of *Poet in the Desert* Wood alludes to his days in the infantry on the trail of Chief Joseph and the Nez Perce. He sees the Indians as, in one sense, favored: "Nature whispered to them her secrets, / But passed me by." "Where," he asks, "are those many-colored cyclones / Of painted and feathered horses / With naked riders, wearing eagle-feathers, / Brandishing rifles, bows, and lynx-skin quivers, / Gleaming through the yellow dust-cloud, / Galloping, circling, hallooing, whooping, / To the War Council?" The answer: "A poor people who asked nothing but freedom, / Butchered in the dark. / In the accusing light of the remorseless Sun / It was not good to see brown boys and girls / Scattered about the grass in Death's repose."

Much of the long poem treats of the plodding pace of the human race toward peace, freedom, brotherhood, and justice, and the Poet's mood oscillates between optimism and despair. In the closing canto, Erskine's radical-reformist proclivity takes over and the Poet calls upon the "dark and brooding angel of Revolution" to "Pitch headlong from the cloudy battlements / And with heavenly fire utterly destroy / This distorted and misshapen world, / That another may rise in beauty, / And the little children be born into joy."

Poet in the Desert calls Walt Whitman to mind. Both poets write in free verse. Both employ alliteration and cataloging. There are filaments of transcendentalism in the poetry of each. Whitman is the great poet of democracy; Wood is more radical in his commitment to what he calls philosophical anarchism. Both Whitman and Wood celebrate love in its various manifestations, but here Whitman is more radical than Wood. Both are poets of the people, speaking forcefully to common men and women. Although both poets are drawn to the natural world, Nature plays a more prominent role in Wood's work and in *Poet in the Desert*; it is usually Nature in spare and austere form. Wood seems to have left no specific acknowledgment of literary debt but his admiration for the Camden poet is apparent in a 1908 short story in *Pacific Monthly*, where, under the pen name Felix Benguiat, he writes: "We have only one poet of our day, only one who is not an echo—Whitman. That is why he is a giant."

Poet in the Desert drew mixed critical comment. Harriet Monroe, editor of *Poetry*, reviewing the 1915 edition in her magazine for September of that year, finds the poem marred by excessive propaganda. But, she writes, "Mr. Wood's special distinction is that he really 'enters the desert,' that his poetry really presents something of the color and glory, the desolation and tragedy, of this wonderland at our western gates." Most of the desert description occurs in the Prologue where, Monroe continues, "no ardor for a Cause gets between the poet and his muse. Therefore, knowing and loving the desert, he gives us something of its varied magnificence in vivid passages of sustained poetic beauty." In Wood, she concludes, "the Far West has produced a poet who, somewhat over-burdened with his message, is capable of rapture; a poet of large vision, of profound sympathy and faith, whose free verse sometimes attains orchestral richness."

A *New York Times* critic calls Wood "a genuine poet and a bold imaginative thinker" with a "style reminiscent both of Walt Whitman and the Hebrew prophets." One reviewer sees *Poet in the Desert* as a series of "rhapsodies and recriminations." Stanley Burnshaw, in *The Masses*, sums up the poem as a "terrifying cosmic outcry against things as they are" (Oct. 1929: 22). In a letter to Erskine, William Allen White writes: "In another day when democracy has served its place . . . some man delving into volumes of forgotten lore will find these songs . . . and will cry 'Here is yesterday singing for today.' "

Excerpts from *Poet in the Desert* appear in literary anthologies compiled and edited by William Rose Benét, Louis Untermeyer, Clement Wood, and others. Almost without exception the selections are drawn from passages describing the high desert country of southeastern Oregon. No other poet has dealt so imaginatively and effectively with this remote corner of the country.

By far the most popular of C.E.S. Wood's books was *Heavenly Discourse*. The dialogues take place in a Dantean heaven with God, Erskine's alter ego, in charge. A battery of characters come and go: Jesus, St. Peter, Gabriel, Rabelais, Voltaire, the Devil, Carrie Nation, Margaret Sanger, Anthony Comstock, Joan of Arc, Mark Twain, Robert Ingersoll, and the battered soul of a Pacifist. Teddy Roosevelt storms heaven as if it were a Cuban hill, eager to arm the angels and fit them with American uniforms. Noah, the drunken mariner, just can't help preferring wine after his experience with water. Anthony Comstock cries in high heaven for just one fig leaf. The humor was not always confined to the conversations: a lady customer, with perhaps unconscious redundancy, asked a San Francisco bookseller where she might find "Celestial Intercourse." The characters discuss fundamentalism, censorship, birth control, love and marriage, imperialism, prohibition, and war. There are forty-one dialogues and the volume concludes with "God's in His Heaven—All's Wrong with the World," a bitter condemnation of what Wood branded as a miscarriage of justice in the execution of Sacco and Vanzetti.

In *Heavenly Discourse* Wood wields a broadsword rather than a rapier, but more than forty printings over the years attest to the satire's persistent popularity.

During World War I when the dialogues first appeared, they generated spirited public response and one of them put *The Masses* off the New York newsstands by beginning with Jesus's query to God: "Father, were you and mother ever married?" One reviewer hailed the dialogues as "the best examples of rough and ready journalistic satire ever published in this country." On the other hand, Vida D. Scudder, professor of literature at Wellesley, huffed:

"the smart and cheap vulgarity of that thing was too much for me."

Although the focus of *Heavenly Discourse* is largely on national or universal issues, now and then, through the voice of Mark Twain, Erskine draws on his experiences in the American West. For example, in canto xxvi, "Censorship," Twain, addressing an assemblage in heaven of God, Bob Ingersoll, Ben Franklin, Carrie Nation, Margaret Fuller, Rabelais, and Voltaire, describes a council on the Sioux Reservation between a commission from Washington, D.C., and the Indians in which the younger braves, angered by the whites' decision to move the Sioux to another reservation, are about to massacre the commissioners. At this point an old chief intervenes, demanding safe conduct for the whites. Mark Twain quotes the chief: "Do you know who I am who say this? I am Spotted Tail, Chief of the Sioux Nation . . . I am a *man*—and if you don't believe it, look at this." He dropped his blanket from his shoulders and lifted into view that which is looked for by every mother . . . to know whether a man child has been born. A moron would have laughed at this phallic gesture, a puritan would have sought a censor—and the police. But the men saved from massacre knew that in a life and death drama it was a solemn testimony of manhood and an appeal to God.

The writing Erskine did in Portland—for the *Pacific Monthly*, for *The Masses* and, with Sara, the re-working of his desert epic— was crowded into a busy professional and public life. In fact, the fullness of his years in Oregon can only be suggested. The practice of law drained time and energy. He was much in demand as after-dinner and public speaker. The Wood household was often the scene of social gatherings. Wood supported progressive political reform. Finally, he spent much of his summers in eastern Oregon riding herd on the vast land grant he was trying to sell. That sale was eventually consummated in 1918. Soon after, Erskine left the law and he and Sara left Oregon for California.

The period from 1918 to 1929 was a productive time for Charles Erskine Scott Wood. In 1918 he published privately *Maia—a Sonnet Sequence*. The work describes and lauds the four seasons; and the influence of Shakespeare, Sidney, and Spenser is evident. Sara wrote two of the sonnets. The next year, *Circe: A Drama with a Prologue* appeared. Maurice Browne and Ellen Van Volkenburg produced Erskine's one-act play, *Odysseus*, in the theater connected with their School of Drama in San Francisco in 1923. A year later Sara and Erskine went on a petit tour to Europe, scouting out the continent as a possible place to live. They soon returned to California and built their house on a hill looking down on the town of Los Gatos. Meanwhile, Erkine was writing and publishing verse, much of it Western, in Harriet Monroe's *Poetry*. Vanguard Press published *Heavenly Discourse* in 1927 and a new edition of *Poet in the Desert* in 1929, substantially expanded and more heavily freighted with ideology than the 1918 version. Also, in 1929, Grabhorn Press of San Francisco brought out a slender volume of Wood's Western verse called *Poems from the Ranges*. There are twenty-two poems in the collection, and except for the initial lyric, "First Snow," Erskine tended to dismiss the cowboy poems as inconsequential. On the other hand, Genevieve Taggard, in the *American Review*, claims that Wood did for the "cowboy and the westerner what Robert Frost has done for the New England farmer" (July-August 1929: 415). Neither judgment is accurate and the poetry deserves a closer look.

Some of the poems are paired in the collection. "Billy Craddock at the Railroad," picturing a cowboy's fright and consternation as a locomotive bears down on him, is matched by the nostalgic and provincial "Billy Craddock in Rome" that begins:

> O, the swallows and the swallows
> Against the sky of Rome;
> And my heart follows
> Away back home
> To the P Ranch on the Blitzen
> And the swallows in the air.

and ends:

> O what to me, by day or night,
> Is old Peter's wart of a dome?
> Squaw-Butte can knock it out of sight,
> Away back home.

In another pairing the poet contrasts the cattle camp as night falls with the awakening camp at dawn:

> Down from the upper dark a night-jar's cry
> Drops like a plummet; the wall of lava rock
> Towers like a fortress frowning on the sky.
> One by one the cattle fold their knees.
> A wakeful cow grumbles deep and low,
> Age-old jungle sound of age-old woe.
> Tinkle of spurs—the night guard.
> Arcturus, great bear warden, torchlike, sweeps
> Upon his watch; the lake is myriad-starred.
> The cow camp sleeps.
> A cuckoo-owl sobs sadly and is still.
> Beyond the outer ramparts of the dark,
> Unhappy, pained, and shrill,
> Coyotes bark.

Later, in the companion poem:

> Dawn creeps like a cripple painfully.
> Cook crawls out to build his sagebrush fire;
> Smoke wreathes through rye grass on the ground,

A dancer whirling filmy skirts around;
The morning blush mounts slowly higher
Until with flame the rim-rock is crowned.
Two yearling bulls butt skulls in mimic fight;
Buzzards and ravens set their funeral sails
For the far marsh; willows are tipped with light,
And in the glowing blue the wan moon pales.

Erskine knew the geology of the Harney Desert, as this little lyric suggests:

On this high mountain cliff,
Which once the sea waves tore,
A fluted shell, petal of a timeless shore.
I shall pass, I and my braggart thought
As dies on space a brazen bell;
But here in the great lap caught
A little fluted shell.

In "Sagebrush," Wood captures the cowboy's love of the Western range:

O I am sick for the sagebrush,
The great, gray sagebrush plain;
And I would give the heart of me
To ride through the sage again.

To feel it scratch my stirrup,
To smell it after rain.
I would give my very heart-blood
For that bitter breath again.

To ride toward the purple hills;
Wind through a tossing mane;
Christ! for a horse between my legs

And the sagebrush once again.

"Lay Me on the Hilltop" is one more expression of C.E.S. Wood's passion for place:

Lay me on the hilltop, close to the sky;
Among the lava rocks let me lie,
Where I've lain in my blanket on the ground;
The big, brown, empty desert all around,
And heard the coyote's crazy howl and cry.
There is the place I want to lie.
I shall not see the slow and lonesome moon;
But still there will be moonlight; still there will be noon.
I shall not hear the furious hoofs, the neigh
Of the wild stallions in their play.
Asleep on the hilltop, next to the sky;
There is the place I want to lie.

Critics agree that "First Snow" is the best of C.E.S. Wood's lyric verse. Genevieve Taggard, writing in *American Review* in 1925, finds it "from the point of perfection and almost primitive directness, one of the biggest poems of this time." An Oregon poet, Verne Bright, in *Northwest Literary Review,* hails it as the finest lyric ever written on the West Coast and "one of the finest in American verse" (July-Aug. 1935: 15). "First Snow" is an appropriate way to take leave of *Poems from the Ranges:*

The cows are bawling in the mountains.
The snowflakes fall.
They are leaving the pools and pebbled fountains.
Troubled, they bawl.
They are winding down the mountain's shoulders
Through the open pines,
The wild-rose thickets, and the granite boulders
In broken lines.

> Each calf trots close beside its mother
> And so they go,
> Bawling and calling to one another
> About the snow.

More than once Colonel Wood was called a cowboy poet. He resented and denied the label. He was neither cowboy nor rancher. But, by virtue of experience, choice, and longtime residence he *was* a Westerner and he knew Indians and frontier troopers, and cattlemen firsthand. Also, he knew and felt the lure of the desert, and the scenic and physical wonders of his adopted region. That knowledge and emotion found impressive expression in the best of his writing.

In 1931, with *Too Much Government,* C.E.S. Wood turned from poetry to prose and from the Western to the national scene. The change was far from felicitous. Wood himself, in a letter to Mark Van Doren, called it "a hack book" that Vanguard Press requested him to write. It is a loose bundle of seven essays on libertarian themes, the most conspicuous of which is a rambling attack on Prohibition and the Volstead Act. Wood homes in on some of the same targets that he attacked in *Heavenly Discourse*—censorship, fundamentalism, and militarism. He decries what he terms a feudal land system in which land is held in fee simple and tends to concentrate in the hands of private corporations. He goes on to deplore corporate control over other natural resources such as coal, iron, and water power. Erskine condemns clear-cut logging in the Pacific Northwest, deals briefly with the suppression of a workers' camp and summer school in southern California that flew the Communist flag and, in the long concluding essay protesting Prohibition, describes the wine-grape-producing environment of California's Santa Clara Valley. Other than these three instances, the American West does not figure in the book.

Both Wood and Vanguard Press were disappointed in the sparse sales of *Too Much Government*, but given its strident didacticism, repetition, and long-windedness, the volume deserved the reception it received. Less invective and more wit would have made a better book.

Although C.E.S. Wood informed Vanguard Press that he was through with prose and would devote himself solely to poetry, such proved not to be the case. As early as May 1932, Vanguard's editor, James Henle, suggested that Erskine write a new volume of satiric dialogues as an updated companion piece to the very successful *Heavenly Discourse*. Wood demurred at first but four years later, in the spring of 1936, he was at work on a new series of dialogues with the setting moved from heaven to earth.

In *Earthly Discourse* (1937), C.E.S. Wood satirizes censorship, 100% Americanism, resistance to birth control, Hearst and Hitler, and defends Edward VIII's right to abdicate the British throne in the name of love and individual freedom. In a lengthy dialogue (nearly one-third of the book) featuring Chief Justice John Marshall and James Madison, Wood writes what amounts to a lawyer's brief that finds no shred of justification in the United States Constitution for giving the Supreme Court the veto power over Congressional legislation. Only two of the eleven dialogues have Western locales: one in Santa Rosa, California, in which American Legionnaires tar and feather a University of California senior for "talking rank Communism on the campus"; and the final piece, "Still in the Jungle," in which God, addressing a company of business tycoons, describes a lovely Western landscape, rich in water, minerals, and forests, and reminds the capitalists that unfettered free enterprise threatens to waste and destroy the natural bounty of the land.

Earthly Discourse went into a second edition and was a better book than *Too Much Government*, but it lacked the brevity, spontaneity, and wit of its heavenly predecessor. It was Wood's last formal publication and popular and critical response alike were lukewarm.

Discussion of C.E.S. Wood as a Western writer would be uneven and incomplete without some consideration of his privately published and even unpublished work in letters and journals. In much of his formal writing Erskine emerges as a sensitive and close observer of nature wherever he finds himself in the West and that might be in a canyon bivouac on the trail of Chief Joseph, in a Portland garden, on the banks of the Metolius River in central Oregon, under rimrock in the Harney high desert, or from the sunny slope of a hill spangled with wild flowers at The Cats looking out across the Santa Clara Valley.

In 1918, Colonel Wood collected seventy-nine sonnets written between 1884 and 1917 and had them privately printed in Portland for distribution among members of his family. About one third are nature sonnets celebrating scene and season, as in the following:

There is a group of oak and beech and pines,
Shady in the day and spicy in the night;
And a walnut, thirsty for the eastern light,
Throws its long leafy arms above the lines
Of trellised fruit trees. When the hot sun climbs
To August noon, this shady grove invites
Me and my book. Here children take delight
And here I watch my brother ant's designs.
Hidden in this dark temple's deepest part
Where robins build and finches grow half tame
A Japan maple spreads its boughs of flame,
A burning altar 'till its leaves depart
One by one; as our hopes leave the heart,
But Spring shall newer buds to life reclaim.

Erskine designated the remaining fifty-three sonnets "Personal." These mark special occasions—birthdays (sometimes his own), departures of children to college, and memories of earlier days. Here is an example of the last category:

Once more I lie upon the grassy spot
Where years gone by, we pitched our summer tent,
My sons and I; it cannot be forgot;
Here was the shaded path by which we went
Down to the little beach and rippled pool
Of our friendly river; strokes our axes left
Where we chopped out a bower in willows cool;
Now silent, of their restless youth bereft,
The sun still shines as bright; the river flows
As murmurous as when it soothed our sleep;
Here was their bed, where the rose-brier grows,
Not anything for long our impress keeps.
They all have gone their ways, and, close to tears,
I muse upon the veiled and hurrying years.

In July of 1921, Colonel Wood visited his Portland family in their summer camp on the Metolius River in central Oregon. There he wrote an extended "Testament" in verse instinct with love for the Pacific Northwest. The opening lines and brief segments here and there attest to his pronounced regionalism.

In the names of all the Pagan gods,
I Charles Erskine Scott Wood
The sole and single of that name
Knowing seventy years of ill and good
Unknown to that Junk dealer Fame,
Though in my youth I, stupid, fought
Wearing the livery of that thing the State
Whose might is by the richest bought

A bully which protects the great;
And served another prostitute the Law
Whose favors are for rich and strong
And now—white-headed last my pen I draw
To write a bit of twilight song.
Make now my last sure will and testament
For that dear and upsprouting brood
My grandchildren in hut and tent
Who share with me this solitude . . . .

* * * * *

To Nancy Honeyman around whose face
Slender and sad cling long curls dark
I leave the peace and quiet of this place:
To her I give some certain beds of mine
Where soft on pine leaves many an hour I lay
My back against a kindly comrade pine
And watched the chipmunks on the logs at play.
To "Buzzy" David Erskine Honeyman
Of the quick smile—I give all, all the flowers
And that's a treasure passing list or plan—
Blue lupins, blue penstemon and after showers
The white orchids each holding at its stem
A moonstone, cardinal flowers and the bright
Indian paint brush and the diadem
Of the cool cloisters Mt. Hood lilies white,
Wild peonies and by the river's brim
Yellow snap dragons—All the flowers and weeds
Unknown of low or late I give to him . . .
To Erskine Biddle Wood, called Erskinson,
I give all trout in the Metolius
The pretty dottings their bright sides upon

And the red streak—the sudden splash and fuss
When quick they show a golden gleaming side
Their quick darting through the waters cool
And the big ones who majestic sullen hide
Each in his own dark ever boiling pool . . .
To Judy—Judith Honeyman I mean,
Though I have had much scorn and ill from her
I give the red top in the meadow green
Through which she rambles like a bee astir
Her small head glowing in the loving sun
A burnished copper ball that roves and roves
Until she comes a clover patch upon
And sucks the big red blooms she dearly loves . . . .

Early in 1923, Erskine and Sara began to keep a large cloth-bound journal in which they might record the march of the seasons and the building of their house, "The Cats," on their thirty-acre hill in Los Gatos. The two poets took a fierce proprietary delight in every flower and bush and bird, every wood rat and lizard, every weed and root and berry that they discovered on their hill; and into the journal, by turns, they recorded their impressions of nature's changing scene. Neither of them was a Californian and so they were unused to the lack of sharp delineation from one season to the next. Sara entered an impromptu verse into the journal that best expresses their perplexity at the way California's seasons are mixed:

> Unbudded boughs
> The wrinkling fern
> Stand side by side.
> The lizard sleeps—
> Robins return.
> Which season lied?

On 20 February 1926, his seventy-sixth birthday, Erskine responded in similar vein by recording in their journal this verse under the title "Beauty Endures":

The Spring is here—The Spring is flying
Buds are bursting—no one grieves
Summer is born when Spring is dying
Beautiful as buds, are leaves.
Summer is here—Summer is creeping
Scarlet stains in her emerald bed.
Autumn awakes when Summer is sleeping,
Beautiful as green, is red.
Autumn is here—O Autumn is banished
Birds fly over—leaves must go.
Winter appears when Autumn has vanished.
Beautiful as leaves, the snow.
Winter is here—now winter is sliding
Down the mountain in foamy suds.
Spring will burst in when winter is hiding.
Beautiful as snow, the buds.

Colonel Wood expresses the same kind of delight in his Los Gatos surroundings in a letter to Mark and Dorothy Van Doren:

Mark's graceful suggestion that the bay leaf—laurel—might adorn my brow led me to bring in from my walk this glorious sunny afternoon a great bough of manzanita—also of the laurel family—I wonder if you poor young things have *ever* passed through grove or whole mountainside of Manzanita in blossom—The pale frosted silver grey leaves just loaded and spangled with the flesh-tinted snow so at a distance one wonders what the warm-tinted delicate drifts are. You pass through such a grove at the last turn of the road to this place—all our own—and the sight of the compact bouquet-like trees—the silver green leaves—the myriad bells hanging crystal white—the perfume and the ground white with fallen pearls and the rich dark mahogany red trunks and limbs smooth as a girl's thigh—is one of the sights of our earthly life.

Forty years after his death at Los Gatos in 1944, there was a rekindling of interest in Portland in Charles Erskine Scott Wood. The revival was sparked by a joint project of the law firm of Wood Tatum Mosser Brooke and Holden and the Oregon Historical Center, seeking perhaps, however belatedly, to honor a prophet who, although he had deserted his own country for California, was to be reclaimed as a proper (some would say improper) Oregonian. At the law firm's instigation and with its assistance, the Historical Center organized an exhibit timed to celebrate the centennial of Wood's entering into the practice of law in Portland in 1884. Until he died at the age of 103, Wood's son Erskine was senior partner. In turn, his son, Erskine Biddle Wood, became head of the firm in 1984. Wood Tatum Mosser Brooke and Holden is believed to be the oldest Oregon law firm continuously to have a partner from the same family. The impressive retrospective entitled "The Legacy of C.E.S. Wood," opened 30 September 1984 and closed 12 January 1985. The exhibit in the Oregon Historical Center consisted of five major displays: the military years at West Point and in the American West; family life in Portland and Los Gatos; Wood as artist and his friendship with J. Alden Weir, Olin Warner, Childe Hassam, and Albert Pinkham Ryder; the law years, contrasting his service to corporate and propertied clients with his support of radical causes; and a final display of Wood's writing, including excerpts from *Poet in the Desert* and *Heavenly Discourse*. Building on the Oregon Historical Center's slender holdings, principal contributors to the show included the law firm, members of the extended Wood clan in Portland and California, the Portland Art Museum, and the Henry

E. Huntington Library, San Marino, California, repository of, by far, the most extensive collection of C.E.S. Wood materials in existence.

Anticipating the opening of "The Legacy of C.E.S. Wood," the Portland press carried several illustrated feature stories on Colonel Wood that for the most part were biographical and anecdotal rather than critical. The best balanced piece was by Keith Moerer in *Willamette Week* (17 Sept. 1984). Walt Curtis, Portland poet and teacher, in *Multnomah Monthly* (Sept. 1984), lamented Portland's neglect of Wood. He stressed the poet's radicalism and Westernness and closed by quoting the last lines from one of Erskine's eastern Oregon range poems, "Billy Craddock in Rome," who preferred Squaw-Butte to the dome of St. Peter. Portland's leading newspaper, the *Oregonian*, also carried a story on Colonel Wood and the exhibit at the Portland Historical Center. Before and after the exhibition Katherine O'Neil and John Miller of the law firm organized a series of round table discussions that met at the Historical Center, bringing together historians, attorneys, poets, artists, and all and sundry who were familiar with Wood or were interested in his extraordinary life and career. One participant in the round table, Tim Barnes, a local writer and teacher of regional literature, recruited a company of actors calling themselves the Heavenly Discoursers and put together a dramatization of selected dialogues from *Heavenly Discourse*. At this writing Barnes's company is still in action. Tim Barnes also published an essay, "Beyond the Bear Paw Mountains: Charles Erskine Scott Wood's Literary Campaign for Freedom," in the Oregon Committee for the Humanities' journal, *Sweet Reason* (Fall 1986). Here Barnes develops persuasively the twin dominant themes in Wood's life and work: freedom and love.

To return to the theme struck early in this essay: Is Charles Erskine Scott Wood a Western writer? It should be apparent at this juncture that the answer must be a qualified yes. He became a Westerner and remained so. But, as in most other aspects of his life, he was a Western writer on his own terms. Erskine received the first and the most profound imprint of the West as a young infantryman on the march through the Harney Desert enroute to Fort Vancouver. That imprint was reinforced in Alaska and then deepened further by participation in the Nez Perce campaign and encounters with the Bannock and Paiute. Wood's early writing that appeared in *The Century* in the 1880s and 1890s and in *A Book of Tales* in 1901 derived from his Army years in the West. When he decided to build a law practice in Portland, he found himself in an urban and valley environment, and yet his responsibility for the wagon road grant drew him back to the high desert summer after summer. That "lean and stricken land" held him in thrall and nourished the creative urge out of which came *Poet in the Desert* and *Poems from the Ranges.*

In the thirty-four years that Colonel Wood lived and worked in Portland, the double dimension in his character and manner of living became increasingly evident. Writing and radicalism went hand in hand with success in corporation law and negotations in buying and selling land. Through his column "Impressions," in *Pacific Monthly*, he emerges as a Western Progressive with a Populist bias that was most evident in his support of Henry George's single tax. He boasted of the beauties of the Pacific Northwest and sought to shape public taste in the sphere of culture, particularly in the field of American fine arts. In 1887, when Stephen Skidmore, a Portland businessman left a bequest to build a fountain in the city, Wood commissioned Olin Warner, his friend from New York days when he was on leave from West Point, to do the job; and today the Skidmore Fountain stands in downtown Portland, an impressive cultural landmark. As one of the founders of the Portland

Art Museum and as a kind of broker in the West representing Eastern Seaboard artists such as Albert Pinkham Ryder, J. Alden Weir, and Childe Hassam, Colonel Wood induced wealthy Portlanders to buy and display the work of leading turn-of-the-century American painters. Add to this Erskine's support and defense of well-known radicals such as Emma Goldman and Margaret Sanger and it is evident that Wood was bent on both refining Far Western tastes and combating the anti-intellectualism and intolerance so often a part of the region's environment. The clearest testimony to C.E.S. Wood's role in shaping the cultural scene in Oregon comes from Harry Corbett, a prominent Portlander, in a letter to Erskine Wood, the Colonel's eldest son:

> I am glad we talked of your father the other day and if we have sense we will do it again on other days and have the memories of him blow the cobwebs out of our brains. He didn't have many cobwebs in his—all was mostly fresh breezes blowing. . . . I know I owe to him most of whatever appreciation I have of fineness and niceties, but, then, hell, the whole of Portland as it once was owes much of its culture to him. . . . There are few who can shape the trend of thought of a whole city. Certainly he did that for this town, and just as certainly that same extraordinary influence of his moved into the most unexpected places: from Mrs. Hanley who never knew how beautiful eastern Oregon was till he brought Hassam out and showed it to her, on to quite a few you and I knew on Burnside St., who revelled in the music of some words he wrote down.

All in all, it might be argued that Wood had as great an impact on Oregon as that far corner of the West had on him.

When Sara and Erskine settled in northern California, he was seventy; but unlike younger writers who, as they aged, lost their leftist leanings and turned sharply to the political right—John Dos Passos and Max Eastman, for example—Wood held fast to his undoctrinaire radicalism. At Los Gatos he deplored the execution of Sacco and Vanzetti, spoke out for Tom Mooney's pardon, worked to prevent deportation of writers deemed subversive, and tried to find a haven for Jewish poets and intellectuals seeking to flee Hitler's Germany. In 1936, at a conference of the newly formed League of Western Writers that included John Steinbeck, Nathanael West, Upton Sinclair, Mike Gold, and Irwin Shaw, among others, Erskine delivered an eloquent address that captured the convention and resulted in his election as the League's first president. Shortly after the convention Colonel Wood condemned Stalin's Moscow purges and came out strongly in defense of Trotsky. Almost to the time of his death, early in 1944, Erskine and Sara were part of a cluster of Western writers and artists at Carmel; and their visitors at The Cats included Lincoln Steffens, Robinson and Una Jeffers, Ansel Adams, John Steinbeck, Yehudi Menuhin, and others.

When all is said, Charles Erskine Scott Wood defies precise classification. He remains a distinct individual who managed to crowd three careers—Army, law, and letters—into ninety-two years of living. Still, the essential quality of the man lies not in his military record, not in his years in the law, not even in his writing. C.E.S. Wood's great force was personal; and to many who knew him he was, in the words of James R. Caldwell, professor of English at the University of California, a kind of "era and a realm."

Selected Bibliography

There is no published bibliography for Charles Erskine Scott Wood. The major collection of manuscript materials is housed in the Henry E. Huntington Library in San Marino, California. There are further significant Wood papers in the Bancroft Library at the University of California in Berkeley, California, and smaller collections in the library of the Oregon Historical Center and in Special Collections in the University of Oregon Library. Wood's son, Erskine, published *Life of Charles Erskine Scott Wood* in a privately printed, limited edition in 1978. The book, as its author acknowledges, is a tribute through reminiscence.

BOOKS BY CHARLES ERSKINE SCOTT WOOD

A Book of Tales. Portland, OR: The Attic Press, 1901. Reprinted under title *A Book of Indian Tales.* New York: Vanguard, 1929.
The Poet in the Desert. Portland, OR: F. W. Baltes P, 1915. Rpt. New York: Vanguard, 1929.
Heavenly Discourse. New York: Vanguard, 1927.
Poems from the Ranges. San Francisco: Grabhorn, 1929.
Too Much Government. New York: Vanguard, 1931.
Earthly Discourse. New York: Vanguard, 1937.
Collected Poems of Charles Erskine Scott Wood. Foreword by Sara Bard Field; Introduction by William Rose Benét. New York: Vanguard, 1949.

WESTERN ARTICLES, POEMS, AND STORIES BY WOOD

"Among the Tlingits in Alaska" (article). *Century Magazine* July 1882: 324-39.
"Death Song of Itsayaya, the Nez Perce" (poem). *Pacific Monthly* Oct. 1900: 275.
"Desert Sonnets" (poem). *Pacific Monthly* Feb. 1910: 133-35.
Orrin Seaman (C.E.S. Wood). "The Deserted Cabin" (story). *Pacific Monthly* Nov. 1910: 486-95.

William Maxwell (C.E.S. Wood). "Drought" (poem). *Pacific Monthly* Aug. 1910: 153.

"The Exhibition of Paintings of Eastern Oregon by Childe Hassam" (article). *Pacific Monthly* Feb. 1909: 141-44.

"A Fallen Pine" (poem). *Poetry, a Magazine of Verse* Feb. 1924: 246-47.

"Famous Indians: Portraits of Some Indian Chiefs" (article). *Century Magazine* July 1893: 436-45.

"First Snow" (poem). *Literary Review* 22 Dec. 1923: 385.

"George Sterling at Our House on Telegraph Hill" (article). *Overland Monthly and Out West Magazine* Dec. 1912: 346.

"An Indian Horse-Race" (article). *Century Magazine* Jan. 1887: 447-50.

William Maxwell (C.E.S. Wood). "Irrigating" (poem). *Pacific Monthly* Aug. 1911: 216.

Felix Benguiat (C.E.S. Wood). "The Juniper Post" (story). *Pacific Monthly* Aug. 1910: 133-37.

"October and Mt. Hood" (poem). *Pacific Monthly* Nov. 1904: 276.

"Portland's Feast of Roses" (article). *Pacific Monthly* June 1908: 623-33.

William Maxwell (C.E.S. Wood). "Pulque" (poem). *Pacific Monthly* Oct. 1910: 367.

Bill Maxwell (C.E.S. Wood). "Seven Pines" (poem). *Pacific Monthly* July 1909: 47-49.

William Maxwell (C.E.S. Wood). "A Song of Cowboys" (poem). *Pacific Monthly* Jan. 1910: 79-80.

"A Song of Summer" (poem). *Pacific Monthly* Sept. 1908: 255.

Felix Benguiat (C.E.S. Wood). "The Toast" (story). *Pacific Monthly* Nov. 1908: 554-63.

William Maxwell (C.E.S. Wood). "The Trooper" (poem). *Pacific Monthly* Nov. 1909: 463.

ARTICLES ABOUT WOOD

Aoki, Haruo. "Chief Joseph's Words." *Idaho Yesterdays* 33.3 (1989):16-21.

Barnes, Tim. "Beyond the Bear Paw Mountains: Charles Erskine Scott Wood's Literary Campaign for Freedom." *Sweet Reason* Fall 1986: 12-22.

Bella, Rick. "C.E.S. Wood." *Sunday Oregonian* 12 Sept. 1984: 1, 6.

Bingham, Edwin R. "Oregon's Romantic Rebels: John Reed and Charles Erskine Scott Wood." *Pacific Northwest Quarterly* July 1959: 77-90.

——————————————. "Experiment in Launching a Biography: Three Vignettes of Charles Erskine Scott Wood." *Huntington Library Quarterly* May 1972: 221-39.

Curtis, Walt. "Charles Erskine Scott Wood: Portland's Radical Philosopher and Bon Vivant." *Multnomah Monthly* Sept. 1984: 8-12.

Moerer, Keith. "The Legend of C.E.S. Wood." *Willamette Week* 17-23 Sept. 1984: 1, 8-11.

Neuberger, Richard L. "C.E.S. Wood Remains a Non-Conformist." *Sunday Oregonian*, Magazine Section 7 Feb. 1937: 9.